A
JOURNEY
THROUGH
A Beautiful Mind

Bianca N. Cotton

ACKNOWLEDGMENTS

For my village handpicked by God who helped me to produce this work out art, thank you!

Preface

A Journey Through a Beautiful Mind was birthed during a time when my thoughts, feelings and emotions began to overwhelm me and I did not know where to store them any longer. Just holding all this information to myself was no longer working for me. Therefore, I discovered poetry to express myself in my rawest form. Before I knew it, poetry became my therapy, just me, my paper and my pen, were sharing our deepest thoughts together. As you continue to read my journey it takes you through my mind, my heart and my soul. The depth of my thoughts exhibits what I thought about my existence and the existence of others around me during a two-year period.

I not only share my thoughts but became a voice for the voiceless. I am sharing their stories as well in hopes that others will start to talk about their journey and free themselves of the burdens that often leave us suffering in silence.

You will notice each section begins with a date because I am taking you on a journey in the order in which my poetry was created. I will not tell it all, you must continue to read to find out.

Love,
Bianca

Table of Contents

JOURNEY THROUGH
November 2010

Poetry Entry: 1

My eyes burn from the tears I cry
When will the pain end?
Matter of fact a better question is when did it all begin?
Did it start by seeing my brothers struggle?
Or watching my mother wrestle with defeat?
Did it start with seeing the black man being the head of the household?
But my mother really was the backbone
Did it start with being mocked, ignored, and pointed at because of hatred?
Or did it start as I witnessed my brother gunned down by another brother because of a street corner?
My eyes burn from the tears I cry
From the injustice
From the helplessness I see in your eye
From my sister being diagnosed with AIDS
From my brother being lost in his rage
When will the pain end
Matter of fact a better question is when did it ALL begin?

Poetry Entry: 2

What does it mean to be FREE?
Is FREE me?
Is free a new form of modern-day slavery?
I am educated but yet shackled by institutional racism
Not smart enuff
Not enuff money
Who eva fed me that lie
Its modern-day slavery
And we mask it by calling it free!
Why must every black boy and black girl work their way up from the bottom
to the top just to start ova?
Why must we keep reINventing the wheel?
Coming from a legacy of struggle and pain
Strength and determination
Resilience and Power
We are yet asking, WHAT does it mean to be FREE?
Well FREE is ME!

Poetry Entry: 3

I am Strong
Being Strong doesn't always mean strength
Sometimes it means being alone
Wrestling with the perils of life when no one is home
Being strong comes with sacrifice
Are you willing to risk your life?...
For me?...for you?...for we?
I am Strong
I have no inner power
Just a mouth that runs 80 miles per hour
"I am Strong"
Is warped into HIS amazing Power that never leaves me alone
NOW I am Strong

JOURNEY THROUGH

November 7, 2010

Poetry Entry: 1

I know why the Caged Bird Sings
It's because she wants to be heard
It's because he wants to be visible
It's because we want to no longer be dehumanized by one another
The oppressor has reached its goal
We are now each other's oppressors
We have internalized, chewed
and spit out the oppression on our brothers and sisters
When will it end?
What will it take?
If I can't be Free, then however will I be me...
Especially when God gave me a Destiny...
When he named me Victory...Not Defeat...Not Hate...Not Self-Destruction
Not Rape
I know why the Caged Bird Sings
It's because she wants to be heard
It's because he wants to be visible
It's because we want to be FREE

Poetry Entry: 2

Am I too critical or am I too analytical
Do my thoughts line up with words?
Do my words affect my behavior?
Am I being too harsh on others because
I am harsh on me
Is it that internal burning feeling of wanting more for myself,
Pushing myself and obtaining Myself and Remaining Myself
How do I share my thoughts without feeling bad about what I said or;
Do I remain silenced in a world that has forced me into silence and expects me to agree?
More and more each day I feel as though my inner rage is going to burst out
And speak loudly of the injustices
That I see,
That I hear,
That I feel

Poetry Entry: 3

The Diary of a Mad Black Woman has begun...
It began long before my birth,
It began when I was stripped of my family,
My faith,
My culture,
And my virginity
This Diary has been in the works for so long that it is finding a voice amongst the crowd
That voice yet struggles to stay alive because
I'm too loud,
Too assertive,
Too manly,
Too aggressive,
Too independent,
Too sassy...
I will not apologize for who I am nor who I will be
I will continue this Diary of a Mad Black Woman on a quest for
Peace,
Love,
And understanding

JOURNEY THROUGH
November 8, 2010

Poetry Entry: 1

You...
You are intelligent
Your spirit gave my spirit the permission to be FREE
To express ALL my thoughts
To do and ask questions later
To stand FEARLESSLY in front of the opposer
You set an example of what it means to develop into a woman from a girl
To stand up for what you believe in always
To never sway or be persuaded by the enemy
You are the epitome of a black woman
That understands her place in society
That has found her voice in the midst of confusion
That is discovering her peace within
That in the mist of misunderstanding you stand firm
You are the budgeter
You turned pennies into dimes
Nickels into quarters
You will turn dollars into millions
You are beautiful because you are
And this is why, I love you

JOURNEY THROUGH

November 14, 2010

ALIVE

Is this how it feels to be alive and not just living
My voice has finally found its way home
My voice is speaking with power and authority that was deeply rooted in me
My voice was scared to show itself because of my past, my misunderstandings and my insecurities
My voice is the leader of today and tomorrow
How can I say it any louder that I am a child of the most high?!
That I am a child from my mother's womb
That I am who I say I am because I am
It feels good to be alive
To feel the earth with my fingers and toes
To smell my flowers
To see my moon
To taste my food
To touch the wind against my cheek
This is what I have been sleeping through
This is what I have been dreaming about
Now it is finally here and here to stay
Here to grow
Here to develop
Here to speak out
I am alive in my soul
My mind
My heart
I feel the adrenaline running through my veins all-the-day long
I am alive
No one can take this away
The power belongs to the most high God
To my Father
To my glistening moon and shining stars

To my deep blue ocean
I love being alive and well
It feels good to feel his arms wrapped around me
It feels great to hear my heart thump at the thought of his name
This is great
It's better than grandma's pound cake
Red lobsters butter biscuits
And granddaddy's BBQ
I'm alive...are you?

Poetry Entry: 2

Grandma's song

Grandma's prayers
Grandma saying, "don't you worry the sun will shine on you"
Was grandma teaching me to deal with my issues
Or was grandma trying to hide me from the pain
Little did grandma know I was experiencing the hurt anyway
Grandma did the best she knew how
But was that what I needed
I wanted grandma to share with me her life struggles,
Her joys and sorrows,
How she overcame it
But it came back to
Grandma's song
Grandma's prayers
Grandma saying, "don't you worry the sun will shine on you"
What I didn't know was grandma didn't deal with her emotionally scarred tissues so it continued to grow until she was covered in scars
What I didn't know was grandma watched her mama do the same thing
Grandma is still waiting for the sun to shine,
The rain to subside
And her internal struggles to evaporate
Little did grandma know, she must forgive herself and begin to heal
Now I tell grandma
Sing your songs
Pray your prayers
And talk to people who have overcome so that you may heal
Now Grandma's songs and prayers are better than ever
And now she shares her struggles with me so that I know that the sun will shine on me soon

Poetry Entry: 4

Why was I stressed?
Was it because I didn't want people to know me?
Was it because I was hiding?
Was it because I realized that being me a Black, Beautiful Woman wasn't
acceptable?
Why was I stressed?
Was it because I never spoke?
I never shared my struggles
I never was vulnerable
How could I have healed without first knowing why I was stressed?
Was I stressed because every eye was on me,
Awaiting me to mess up
To get pregnant
To point out one of my flaws
Why was I stressed?
Was it because I knew better but didn't know how to do better?
Was it because I liked doing the things I was doing but expected different
results?
Was it because I couldn't hear what he said?
Or couldn't fathom the reasons why I was in the situation I was in because I
placed myself there?
Why was I stressed?
Because my soul wasn't being fed and it was drowning in uncertainties,
mistrust, misguidance and ignorance
Was it because I cared to know my history, but didn't know my history?
Was it because people were lying to me to keep me from knowing the "truth"?
What happens to the truth shall set you free?
Why was I stressed?
Because I wasn't truly free
Socially
Emotionally

Physically
Spiritually
Economically
Racially
Am I totally free now
NO
Because the more I fight the harder the leash gets to let me know that I am
not free
I am free emotionally, spiritually, and mentally
But I am still fighting for equality
All I want is free speech
Free press
Free petition
And the Assembly
That is FREE to me
No policy holding me back
No subtle racism
No gender gap in pay
Opportunities for all
When that day comes I will be 100% Free

Poetry Entry: 5

I see you, even when you think no one is looking
I see your sad countenance
I see your tear stained pillow
I see you holding your head down in shame
I see you asking why this had to happen like that
What you don't see is me watching you
I see you get mad every time someone mentions your past
It hurts even more because you are attempting to cover it up with solutions without
dealing with the issue
I see the pain in your peepers when you look at me
Asking me why
What if...
I wonder....
What really matters...
I see your temple, but what is inside
Who are you?
What do you want?
How can I assist you on this straight and narrow path that many fall on and off?
What will it take for you to see yourself?
What will it take for you to see your temple?
What will it take for you to open your peepers and see your past, your reality and
your destiny
I know you better than you think I do
Because I am you
I have walked down your street
In your shoes
With your book bag full of desire
I see you
Because I am looking at me
Through this mirror of hope and prosperity
Through this mirror of self-worth, self-determination and admiration
Through this mirror I see you and your family I see you

Poetry Entry: 6

Sometimes I just want you to listen
Not to speak
Sometimes I just want to express how I feel about the situation
Not looking for no advice or next steps
Sometimes I just want you to feel what I'm telling you, for you to just nod your head in understanding
In agreement
In support
Sometimes I don't want you to say anything about what I'm telling you
Just listen
Just digest what I'm saying
Just let me vent
Let my therapy be me hearing you breathe as I pour my heart out so that I may be filled again
All I want is for you to listen and listen carefully
Give me eye contact
Turn your head in my direction
Turn your body towards mine and listen
I just want you to feel what I'm saying
Then if you have a thought, a but, a comment you can save it 'til I'm done
Because the interjections stop the flow of my energies
Then I lose what I am saying and forget about what I was thinking and must start from point A to reach Point Z again
Just Listen
Then speak if need be

Poetry Entry: 7

Why do you scream my name?
Can't you see I'm talking to someone
Instead of you tapping me on the shoulder
Holding up your arms
And welcoming me with a big hug
You choose to scream my name
Only being two feet away
Once again you place yourself in this situation to be ignored
I turn around to say hello and go right back to my conversation
I know you know you were being rude
But you don't care
You want to see me act a fool
Guess again
I will not put on a show for you
It's not worth my time to even stoop to your level and explain to you what I
mean
Are you serious?
You haven't learned your lesson yet
Maybe one day you will
When you learn to approach me because I have tried to tell you before
But did you listen
NO
It went in your right ear
And came out of your left one
One day you will understand what I mean; when I say SCREAMING my name
when I'm talking is rude
One day you will understand why I laugh when you do that
One day you will understand why I look at you the way I do
The Lord is not through with me yet
And yet you continue to try me
Amen for grace and mercy because I need it
Let you scream my name one more time when I'm talking

I pray for my spirit meat to touch your spirit
And not my flesh
Amen

Poetry Entry: 8

I always wanted a mentor
Someone who would be there for me
A shoulder to lean on
An ear to hear
A woman or man who would be my "Superman"
I continuously looked for this mentor
This role model,
Later I found out I had mentors
Role models
And the greatest of them all, Jesus
He showed me every way to turn
Every mountain to climb
Every single piece of advice came from Him
And through his people
I really found a mentor in me
All along I was searching for this magical being
And it was in me
I was looking for the Holy Mary and she was in my face
How could I have not seen her?
Paid any attention to her
Because all along I was looking at the wrong one
Each and every person was a reflection of me
My past
My present
And my Future
I am glad that I finally found her because she is my inspiration
It was a divine appointment that I could not miss
I arrived on time
Right in time for this grand occasion
Known as life
The life that is bountiful
The life that is miraculous

The life that is blissful
Life is good as I know it
This life is worth living; adding to the path that was laid long before me
Long before my mother knew me
Long before my name existed
This life is full of surprises
Keep living and ye shall find exactly what you've been looking for and more

Poetry Entry: 9

As I sit in silence
I hear myself think
I talk to myself
Silence is good
I am not distracted by any noise
It's just me and my thoughts
I think this is how God intended it to be so I can hear him
So, we can get to know each other better
I'm liking this
I sit in silence, with my thoughts and I write
I finally get to type my thoughts on my computer without distraction
I hear myself say
I like this...this peace and tranquility that transcends the four walls of my
dorm room in the middle of corn fields
I like getting to know myself better
The time is now for introspection
Reflection
And Education
The education of BNS
I am learning from my successes and lessons learned
I am learning from my brothers, mothers and fathers that set examples for me
Good ones and not so productive ones
I am learning to listen to my heart
So that I can find my true love
So, I am listening to my heart
That was the key to unlock my true love
Looking at myself is not so bad after all

Like India I'm having a *Private Party*

"Ain't nobody here but me, my angels, and my guitar singin' baby look how
far we've come here
I'm havin' a private party
Learning how to love me
Celebrating the woman I've become, yeah

Sometimes I'm alone but never lonely
That's what I've come to realize
I've learned to love the quiet moments
The Sunday mornings of life
Where I can reach deep down inside
Or out into the universe
I can laugh until I cry
Or I can cry away the hurt"
As I sit in my peace and tranquility
I appreciate me more
I love me more
I am grateful for me more

Poetry Entry: 10

Why don't you cover your mouth when you sneeze?
Don't you know you spreading your germs to me?
Did you look at me and ask my permission to cough on me?
That's the least you can do if you refuse to cover your mouth with your sleeve
Man, I wish more people covered their germs with the thought of protecting others in mind
Can we all learn to be respectful of each other's space especially in public places?
Why don't you cover your mouth when you sneeze?
You think the wind is going to take it away on an imaginary cloud that has anti-bacterial hand sanitizer on it
I don't think so
It's all a figment of your imagination
Please come back to reality
Do you know you making me sick, literally?
I can respect you sick but I would like it if you covered your germs
Don't be spreading your germs no more
I told everyone about you
When they see you coming they run
Because they have been warned
And so were you
But you refuse to take the advice given to you
Remember to cover your mouth because it's the right thang to do

Poetry Entry: 11

Ummm relationships
It has great moments
It has rollercoasters
It has sunny days
It has thunderstorms
When people ask me how are we doing
Sometimes I wanna tell them the truth
I don't know
I haven't spoken to him over the phone in a while
Texting doesn't count
Sometimes I wanna say
I wish I knew because I wanna know too
I can't provide myself with a report from our last convo a week ago
That's old news
What's new
What's happening
I continue to ask myself this question
I wonder if I am I being an enabler by calling him when I was awaiting a
callback
Am I doing too much
What is too much I don't know yet
Do I feel like he's been pulling his weight most of the time?
Ummmm that's a good question
Maybe the real question is what are our roles in each other's lives?
How do we help one another?
Is there a measuring stick for it?
No
I don't want it to be
I want to feel like my share is being complemented by his
Is this how marriage is going to be?
He runs away for a few days and then returns like he never left
That ain't cool

I want someone who is consistent
Effectively communicates with me no matter what is going on
Is that too much to ask for?
It's the simple things that make me smile
I see a crack in our foundation
It was hiding beneath all the glitz and glam
It was hiding beneath what I didn't want to see
It was hiding in the "I'm sorries," "I feel bads," "I wish I wouldas"
It was hiding beneath the "I love yous"
It was hiding within those long walks near the lake
It was in the way you don't say things
What I wanna know is how did you grow up?
Did your daddy do that to your mama?
The apple doesn't fall too far from the tree
Where did you learn this?
Because it is time to unlearn this type of communication style if we are going
to prosper together
I'm tired of saying this over and over again for the past nine months
I know you gonna say "I waited seven years for you"
ok cool
we need to build on the past not revert to it
You feel me?!

Poetry Entry: 12

To my sister,

I have no clue how it feels to lose a mother
I cannot fully understand your pain
I am here to say that I am praying for your strength in this time of sorrow
That tomorrow may not be easy and your burden may feel heavy
Just know that my heart is beating for you
That my heart is caring for you
That my soul is grieving for you
You may feel as if no one understands your tears
Just know that God will be all you need
He is your comforter
He is your rock
And he will be there for you when no one else will
I hope you find peace in this storm
And tranquility within this night
May God's presence be so strong that you can't let go

Love You,
Bianca

JOURNEY THROUGH

December 7, 2010

Poetry Entry: 1

I write what I like
I write how I feel
Sometimes I even write my deepest thoughts that may provoke you
I write what I don't like
Like that paper assignment that seems very simple but is complex due to the
intricacies of the professor's objectives, questions, wants and needs
I write until my head explodes with words, sentence structure, more course
material and transition words
Then it comes to a point in which I burn out and do not know what is left to
say, add or revise
I write until my fingers are numb and my wrist is throbbing with pain that my
forearm says, "no more" to
I wish I could write more about how I feel when I feel and let that be
Only in my dreams will that be an assignment with my own objectives and
turn it in for a grade to be critiqued by me
I write because I like the feeling off weight lifting from my shoulders as if an
eagle is soaring high above the clouds that are no longer in sight
Now my words must be formed into complete sentences that no longer run-on
nor are fragmented due to incomplete thoughts
I endure the red ink marks on my paper that looks like an art project gone
wrong
I read the comments with pause only to revise them and see similar comments
on the final
I swallow the grade like the whale swallowed Jonah—whole
For this reason, I write what I like when I am not consumed with what's
incumbent

Poetry Entry: 2

Lord,
I feel so amazing today
As a child, you told me to dream and dream big
Back then my big dream was to go to college and succeed
Not only for myself but for my family my friends my Lord
I feel like I can fly
Like my wings are the wingspan of an eagle that will soar high but will not forget about what is low
I used to dream Big and thought what if that happens to me
What if I was on the tv screen
What if I was the one Black face you see on a college brochure one day
You know you heard my thoughts
My "what ifs"
My "I wonders"
Today I stand to say that you heard me all along and knew I feared your answers
Because my what ifs turned into "Now what?"
And my "I wonders" turned into "What's next"
I keep dreaming Big
You continue to show me yourself and your capabilities so that I may follow suit and be a heart like you that pumps the blood into the veins
So that I may be the diamond-like you that shines after the pressure was applied
I will go as high as you want me to go
I will soar as long as you want me to soar
And I will continue to pay attention to my thoughts because one day they may come true
And I will be in awe again with you

Poetry Entry: 3

I love—how you love
I love how you love me unconditionally
You look past my faults and see me
You see your creation and waiting for me to reach my next destination
To live in my destiny
So that you can elevate me
And reveal to me more of why you created me
To be in a place where no one likes me
Likes the truth
They don't even like you
But they say they love you and you are their everything
I see everything but you
But that's why you love unconditionally
We were saved by graced and mercy was our gift that keeps on going
I love—how you love
How can I love like that?
You have always told me to be patient, kind, long-suffering and to keep no record of wrongs
I know I need help
My patience is wearing thin and my list is starting to overflow
I need a detox quick before I have no more life to live
Jesus continues to teach me how to love just like you
So that I may live my destiny to the fullest
I appreciate your listening ear
And your gentle touch
Thank you again for teaching me how to love

Poetry Entry: 4

Senioritis
Does it have its arms around me
Wrapped really tight
I think I just realized that May 1st is getting closer and closer to the day and
I'm still working on my personal statement
This is ridiculous
Senioritis has knocked on my door
I asked who is it
And opened the door looking for somebody
It crept in without a sound
I did not see it coming
But I know its here
How long will it stay
He said he wants to stay the whole year
I can't have you in my home that long
You must go as soon as possible
Pack your bags and leave the same way you came
Senioritis does not want to leave
I tell it every day that it must go
But I haven't opened the door so that it can creep back out the way it came

JOURNEY THROUGH

December 17, 2010

Poetry Entry: 1

He gave me life
So why aren't I living it
To the fullest
To reach my fullest potential
To tap into my destiny
This is the reason he died on Calvary
So that I may be set free
And live life more abundantly
And yet I put myself back into a box when I get scared
And yet I say that ain't for me
Maybe for you
This is not living my life to the fullest
So, on today I walk with my head held high
With my best attitude on
And the perfect smile
That says I am fearfully and wonderfully made
In the image of the Great Man that took time to create me
Shape me
And Raise me
Into what He wanted for me
This is the day that I begin to live
And breathe
Sing
And have few needs
Because it's not about me
But about His Destiny

Poetry Entry: 2

I have risen above my circumstances
My environment does not have a say in who I will be
Just because I was born on the South Side of Chicago
Raised in Drexel View
Does not depict who I will be
Due to the negative associations with my neighborhood and its people
I have risen above my circumstances
Because of my faith
Determination
Support from family
I know that there is more to life than just the four corners of my block
There is a life to be lived past Drexel Blvd
Past the fourth ward
Past the drug dealers
And crack heads living
I am a product of my environment in reverse
I smile everyday
Because every day is a new chance to take risks
I walk with my head held high
Praying that I am a light that will shine in the midst of darkness
That my life will speak volumes to other young girls and boys that think that college
is an abstract thought
I speak to my people because we are hurting from self-oppression
Self-destruction
And for a lack of knowledge we do perish
We are falling too because of basement thinking
Low-self esteem
Seeing no way out of our created misery
The time is out for self-pity
I am a product of my environment in reverse
I will continue to push past the expectations placed on me
Because only God is in total control of my Destiny

Poetry Entry: 3

To my NUMBER ONE Fan
Thank you for standing by my side through the thick, the thin, the pretty and
the ugly
You have been the inner voice for me when I was speechless
You have walked in my shoes when I did not want to put them on
You have been the smile on my face when I wanted to cry
Thank you for being my NUMBER ONE fan that has always been in the stands
Now your encouragement
Positivity
Boldness
Beauty
Has rubbed off on me
You have told me that if I believe then I can achieve
If I think it then I will do it
Thank you for being my motivator in the times of need
To my NUMBER ONE Fan, thanks for being me
As I look into the mirror
I know that you are still there and will not disappear
As I travel from here to there you are always with me
Never leaving me as long as I feed you with positivity
To my NUMBER ONE Fan, ME!

JOURNEY THROUGH

December 16, 2010

Poetry Entry: 1

<u>I am No Ordinary Woman</u>

I am No Ordinary Woman
I will take a stand in the midst of fear
Today I take the shackles off myself
Today I come out of this box that I once called my home
I am unwrapping my gifts
Dusting them off
Polishing them like never before
No Ordinary Woman I am
I am SUCCESS
S-U-C-C-E-S-S
I am
My attitude equals my altitude
So that means I must soar with the eagles and not walk with the turkeys
I am not afraid to take a stand
To stand out amongst the crowd and be seen for who I am
So that the shoes that I am destined to walk in
Run in
Speak in
Dream in
Jump in
Will free another sister, brother, mother or friend
From being in the box that they created for themselves
I shall take a stand against my biggest hindrance
ME
Fear builds walls and I'm building bridges
Because I am No Ordinary Woman
Who has a Vision

JOURNEY
THROUGH
December 30, 2010

Poetry Entry: 1

All he wants for Christmas is you
All he wants is his parents' tender love and care
I wait for the day to see my father get the gift that he has been adamantly
persistently seeking after since 2004
All he wants for Christmas, for New Years, for the rest of his life is you
Your motherly love
Your motherly understanding
Your motherly advice
What he is getting is not helping him to grow as a person and fulfill his
destiny
Due to his dwelling on the fact that he is being ignored and talked about
without him at the table
All he wants for Christmas is you
All he wants is for you to be real with him
Honest with him
Not fearful of him
This is your eldest son
That seeks to have your love and your love more abundantly without terms
and conditions attached to it in small print
All he wants for Christmas is a family with no secrets, no sneaking and no
stubbornness
All I want for Christmas is to see this cycle of misunderstandings, fear, lack of
trust, spitefulness, jealousy, envy, anger, and judging end today
Jesus died on the cross to save us and yet we are killing ourselves and not
using our family as a place of refuge but rather as a battleground

Poetry Entry: 2

As I look into the mirror what do I see
I see a girl inside of me
A girl that's full of curiosities
A girl that's full of majestic dreams
Only God knows her true heart
Even before she starts to ponder
Feel
React
Respond
Reflect
This is the girl in the mirror that dreams bigger than the room she lives in
Bigger than the 13-story building she resides in
Wider than a millionaire dollar smile
This girl is bursting with ideas, thoughts and drive that it cannot be contained to the four corners of a room
I will continue to see the girl in the mirror because it is me

JOURNEY THROUGH

April 4, 2011

Poetry Entry: 1

The Levees Broke...
My heart breaks for you
I feel compassion filling my body like Hurricane Katrina breaking the levees
It came over me like a powerful wind pushing the waters
The tears just continue to roll down my face without my permission
Not one tear asked me if it was ok for them to escape the quiet place that not even I wanted to feel
Because I knew the levees would break and continue to flow from my insides to the outside and expose me like my brother who was stripped naked and sold on the auction block
I can no longer hold the wall that was blocking the overflow of compassion, heartbreak, sorrow, empathy and just plain brokenness that lies within
Now I lay open and vulnerable to you and Daddy
I feel His covering
His love
and know that His Mercy and Grace is sufficient for you
Now is the time to Hope Again
Live Again
Breathe Again
And Move forward dropping the loads of yesterday and today and not picking up the ones that tomorrow will present

Hey love,

We are a little past the half way mark on this journey through a beautiful mind. It's time to pause, let's reflect on which poems stirred something in you. What was stirred up inside of you? Why do you think these thoughts, feelings or even memories rose?

Share your thoughts below.

JOURNEY THROUGH
September 22, 2011

Poetry Entry: 1

It saddens me to see our Black boys lynch themselves
By hanging out on the streets
Late at night
Dealing drugs
Getting blown
Raising attention to themselves so that the police get involved to solve their problems for them
Why is it that our Black boys seem to be lost and think it's better to start college and stop to come back home to make money and possibly never return?
Why is it that our Black boys think it's cool to disrespect and threaten our Black girls to feel like they are in control?
It saddens me to see our Black boys stand against police cars, hands behind their backs with handcuffs squeezing the life out of their wrists
It saddens me to even know that some of our Black boys think that this is the only path they can have in life is a path of self-destruction rather than life and life more abundantly

JOURNEY THROUGH
September 28, 2011

Poetry Entry: 1

I don't know how to read
Who is there to help me?
Who even knows that I suffer silently in this prison they call a school?
Sitting in my cell that they call a classroom
And getting further behind the bars that they call academics
I don't know arithmetic
How do I do '9-3'?
What does that equal?
IDK
I never knew!
But my teacher pats me on the back and pass me to the next grade
Before I know it, I'm graduating from elementary school and yet lost and stuck in second grade where I was left to die mentally
I don't have a Spanish textbook neither does my teacher know Spanish
How must I learn to communicate Spanish if I don't even know my ABCs in Espanol?
Who can I run to,
To fulfill my needs that aren't met within these four walls we call the education system?
We shall overcome someday

JOURNEY THROUGH

September 30, 2011

Poetry Entry: 1

Who Am I?
I am the daughter of the Most High
I am Bianca Nina Spratt
Born to a mother and father and two brothers
I am a proud auntie, cousin, friend, sister, daughter, lover
I am on a spiritual and historical journey to truly understand where I came from so I know where I am going
I am a speaker
I am a trailblazer
I follow Jesus, my heart and first mind
I am full of joy and happiness
I am confident
What I want to become?
I want to become what God has destined me to be
I want to be a businesswoman, entrepreneur, community organizer, youth development specialist
I want to be done wearing masks altogether
I want to be me all the time no matter what
I want to continue to take risks
I have no limits on me

JOURNEY THROUGH
November 26, 2011

Poetry Entry: 1

My heart cries for you
My soul aches for you
You are so precious and tender
You are so special you have your own set of directions on how to care for you
Like dry clean only clothing
I will sacrifice for you, to protect you for as long as I can
I pray that God's hand is on you as you walk to school alone
Do your homework
Jump the fence to get in the place you call home
How dare your mother says, "Let her jump the fence"
When its slippery, raining and dark out here
I couldn't let you do that
My heart isn't into
Neglect
Child abuse
Or any other form of mistreatment you go through
When I see you I see light, intelligence and decisiveness
I love you just the way you are
You two are my turtle doves that are as white as snow on a winter's night
I wish you sweet dreams
Maybe one day my heart won't cry from the pain you experience because it will be over and
you two will fly high with all positivity under your wings and shake adversities off you; I wait for each time we meet and I see your smile and all those pretty teeth
When I see you, I see me and we can make it together

Poetry Entry: 2

I came back to Chicago for you
I wanted our relationship to grow and mature
I wanted you to have a refuge and a place to recharge your batteries for strength
I admire your courage
Your determination
Your know how
I enjoy every waking moment that I'm with you
And I will not compromise our time together for no one or thing
I love you that much and my love for you grows stronger each day
I came back to Chicago for you
Because I know you need positivity
Encouragement
Kind words
And exposure to different things in your life
I pray that God continues to bless me so I can bless you
I pray that God blesses you so you can bless others too
I came back to Chicago
Because I know you needed to see someone who resembles your father
Who talks about your father
I know you hurt but I hope I can help alleviate some of this pain that may keep
you up at
night
Have you worried
And dismayed
I pray that you soak up all this goodness that is at your fingertips
And not be swayed by the darkness that preys
I came back to Chicago for you because
I wanted our relationship to grow and mature

JOURNEY THROUGH

December 2, 2011

Poetry Entry: 1

I Am...

I am whoever I say I am if I wasn't then why would I say I am
I am a Beautiful Black Queen surrounded by my brothers and sisters from other mothers
I am inclusive in my approach to life
I am victorious and will always have the victory
I am proud and thankful to be a child of God
I am a sister, auntie, cousin, granddaughter, friend and niece forever
I am a motivator, encourager, speaker, teacher and listening ear
I am a shoulder to lean on
I am the spine of your book
I am the title of your chapter
I am the stone in your building
I am the emergency light on the stairwell
I am the tear you cry
I am the North Star in the sky
I am whoever I say I am if I wasn't then why would I say I am

JOURNEY THROUGH
February 23, 2012

Poetry Entry 1:

I'm birthing this dream and it's hard to conceive
I'm birthing this dream and my heart is trying to conceive
I'm birthing this dream and my mind is trying to conceive
All the wonders and treasures that God has stored up for His people
A seed was planted in me
Before my very existence
Before my mother could say no more children are coming out of here
Before Adam had Eve
Before Cain killed Abel
I mean this seed was small in size but mighty in power
There were no other thoughts of me before His
He had the greatest plan for me before I could even say His name, Jesus
The only man I know that could save me
Raise me
And fill me up with His love like no other man I know
His seed in me is beginning to grow and recognize its strength and power in
Him
I mean my arms are tightening up
My core is flattening
My legs are regaining its strength
My feet are planted in solid ground
My head is pointed in the right direction to go higher and remain humble in
You
My seed is an inch bigger
A centimeter thicker
And has more spots on it from the battle wounds that represent my fight,
My struggle
And my tenacity to stay in this race that is not given to the swift
Nor to the strong
But those who endure to the end
His seed in me is beginning to grow and I am recognizing the responsibility
that comes along with this seed

JOURNEY THROUGH

October 10, 2012

Poetry Entry: 1

Whoever said young black ladies didn't want the best out of life?
Whoever said they didn't have goals and aspirations?
Whoever said they too can't be leaders?
Well I'm here to say and prove that you are wrong and continue to spread
lies
I am the girl who wakes up and goes back to sleep and is late to the first
period
I am the girl who can't stand my teacher because she doesn't like me
I am the girl who asks questions because I want to know, not to be funny and
get punished for it
I am the girl who is a leader but uses my influence for negative behavior
I am the girl who's tired after 8 hours of school, two hours of afterschool,
three hours of homework, six hours of sleep to do it all over again
I am the girl who wears pearls as part of a trend but doesn't know the real
meaning
I am the girl on the bus catching an attitude with the bus driver and gave her
a piece of my mind
I am the girl who can't figure out how to talk to my parents
I am the girl who gets straight A's without much hard work
I am the girl who struggles, cries, laughs, lies, searching, seeking, praying,
weeping, preserving, dominating, irritating, ovulating
I mean I am the girl who everyone wants to be around, emulate, duplicate
I am the girl who is confident, powerful and brilliant, wise beyond my years
due to my life experiences and common sense that is not common to you
I am that girl
Whoever said it couldn't be all of this in me?

ABOUT THE AUTHOR

Bianca is an author and entrepreneur based out of the South Side of Chicago. With a heart for women and a heart for encouraging the hopeless, Bianca launched Behind the Confident Smile, a movement, and organization dedicated to dealing hope to women while they walk in love and heal from past hurts. Most importantly helping women to restore not only their smiles but their confidence in themselves.

We want to hear from you, email us at Hello@behindtheconfidentsmile.com and share your stories about how A Journey Through A Beautiful Mind blessed you.

Journal

It is your turn to share your voice using the written word. You have a story you can share with the world. Your story can help someone else overcome a challenge, get through a rough season in life and even spread joy. There are questions here to help you jumpstart telling your story.

We want to hear from you, please submit your stories to Hello@behindtheconfidentsmile.com.

Question 1. What's been your greatest challenge in life? Why?

_____

_____

_____

_____

_____

_____

_____

_____

Question 2. What do you love about you? Oftentimes we focus more time on what we do not like about ourselves. I want to challenge you to focus on what you love about you. Share in detail and why you love this aspect of you.

_____

_____

_____

_____

_____

_____

_____

_____

_____

_____

_____

_____

_____

_____

Question 3. Do you love who you were created to be? Write a love letter to yourself. Give it to a trust loved one and ask them to return the letter to you when you need it most.

_____

_____

_____

_____

_____

_____

_____

_____

_____

_____

_____

_____

_____

Question 4. What do you want to celebrate? Write about the most recent time where you were proud of you.

_____

_____

_____

_____

_____

_____

_____

_____

_____

_____

_____

_____

Question 5: What do you want to write about? Create your own question and flow with your creative self. You are amazing!

_____

_____

_____

_____

_____

_____

_____

_____

_____

_____

_____

_____

_____

96977860R00045

Made in the USA
Lexington, KY
25 August 2018